# THE SPEECH TEACHER'S HANDBOOK

## A PARENT'S GUIDE TO SPEECH & LANGUAGE

### MOLLY DRESNER, MS SLP-CCC

To Alex,

"whatever is done by only me is your doing, my darling"

—E.E. Cummings

# ACKNOWLEDGMENTS

A very special shout out goes to all of the families that I have had the privilege to work with. Thank you for welcoming me onto your team. I love every minute of working with you and your children. You hold a very special place in my heart.

A gigantic thank you to my family and friends who are family. I appreciate your endless support, advice, and love. I am forever grateful for your responsiveness to every phone call, text, and email throughout the day.

To all of my professors, supervisors, colleagues and SLP loves, thank you for sharing your wisdom and strength. You inspire me on a daily basis and I have learned so very much from each of you. Phyllis, you are my role model and I am eternally thankful for all that you have taught me.

Thank you to Bernadette Murphy for editing this handbook and providing creative insight. Thank you to Kent Bingham who made this labor of love come to life. Thank you to Justin Pike for your beautiful designs—your talent is magic.

Thank you to the brilliant folks at Clyde Group. You have provided me with an incredible amount of guidance and encouragement throughout this process. I am so appreciative that you have held my hand each step of the way.

# Table of Contents

# Introduction

ello! The fact that you picked up this handbook tells me you probably live with a little one who is having a hard time communicating. If so, you have come to the right place! This handbook is designed so that you can read it in one or two sittings and then immediately begin to help your child improve his or her communication skills. The book will give you fun and functional suggestions for improvement and a host of activities to choose from that are easy and natural to incorporate into your daily routine.

As a speech language pathologist, I am often asked by parents and caregivers, "What can I do to help my child?" This easy-to-read, easy-to-follow guide is my answer to that question. You are with your child the most and see her in a variety of different contexts. You know what he's like at home, how she plays at the park, what he says (or doesn't say) at the doctor's office, at daycare or school, and in the car/train/bus. Together, we will work to help her communicate better, no matter where you are.

The idea for the booklet came about when I realized that we each hold a unique piece of the puzzle. You know your child best and how most easily to work with her. With years of experience working with little ones, I bring proven techniques for improving his speech and language skills. Working together, we can make great strides in helping your child communicate effectively and easily.

This handbook is meant to serve as a reference as well as a resource for tried-and-true speech therapy tips. Please note, however, that this handbook is not meant to be a substitute for traditional speech therapy or a "quick fix." If you believe your child needs a speech language pathologist, please consult with your child's pediatrician or teacher.

# My Story

I am a speech language pathologist who found my niche working with children under the age of five. It is truly a privilege to teach children how to communicate and I take my role of advocate very seriously. By advocate I mean that when I am clinically engaged with helping a child, I am that child's voice until he is able to communicate independently. When I work with families, I insert myself into their daily routine. I come to the house and sit on the floor. I join in any activity that she is playing and provide parents with tips and tricks on how to make that activity more "speechy." I listen, observe, and provide insight in order to become a true member of the team.

As much as I wish I could be in every living room, on every floor, working with every child—I simply can't. I created this handbook in hopes that my words can reach as many families as possible.

# In case you are interested in the nitty-gritty...

I am a nationally certified speech language pathologist. I hold a Certificate of Clinical Competence (CCC) from the American Speech and Hearing Association (ASHA). Additionally, I am a certified Teacher of Students with Speech and Language Disabilities (TSSLD). I completed my master's degree in Speech & Language Pathology at Teachers College, Columbia University and my bachelor's degree in Speech and Hearing Science at The George Washington University.

# The bottom line:

My career has been dedicated to pediatric speech and language. I have worked in a variety of environments including home and community-based settings, daycares, preschools, and hospitals. I am passionate about involving family members in the therapeutic process and I recognize the value of empowering the individuals who care for the child on a daily basis.

Each and every day, my goal is to help you help your little one communicate.

## Let's get started.

# Principle #1
## Baby Steps Are The Biggest Steps

I t is a biological urge to want your child to be the smartest, brightest, happiest kid in the room. You are her biggest fan, and you should be. It is important for you to be his first cheerleader, so that he gains confidence in his own actions down the line. Additionally, it is important to realize that "baby steps" are appropriately named. Your baby, from birth up until five years old, is literally changing and growing in the most incremental ways each day.

Therapists are hypersensitive to every single, almost undetectable thing that your child is doing. We are always "on" and keeping track of the differences that are occurring in your child's ability to understand others and express her wants and needs. And you should not be! Please do not expect that of yourself.

But it's very important to find satisfaction in small changes. Every one of them is incredibly important to the learning process. So take each step as it comes and please, do not skip steps. That makes it harder for your child and will only cause frustration.

One of life's mysteries is how the majority of children learn language so quickly and seamlessly. Especially a language like English, which is full of exceptions to the rule. As much as every single child is different and unique, more often than not, they are all trekking through the various stages of language learning together. That is, your baby is going to start to make sounds based on happiness (coo sounds, gurgle sounds, giggles,) and not-so-happiness (cries and whines) before he babbles. Children are going to babble sounds before they start to produce what we call jargon. Jargon is when your child says a string of syllables that sound like gibberish with appropriate inflection, as if she's speaking in her own little language. He is going to produce jargon as he begins to say those first few words. And she will produce roughly 25-50 single-word productions (mama, dada, baba, ball, up, more, juice, etc.) before she starts to combine those words ("more juice" "mama up" etc.)

# WE HAVE TO KNOW WHAT WORDS MEAN BEFORE WE CAN USE THEM

In working with children who struggle with communication, it's often that receptive language—our child's understanding of language—is overlooked. It's important to remember that these receptive skills come first! Your child needs to be able to understand what is being said, before he will be able to use language to communicate.

For example, if you ask your child to "find the ball" and she doesn't know what a ball is or where to look for it, then she is not ready to say the word "ball." Children need to know the names of things in their environment before they will be able to label them. By six months, your baby will be responding to new sounds in the environment, voices, music, and his or her name being called. As your child grows, he should be able to follow basic directions with gestures for support (e.g. pointing to the object while saying, "pick it up;" putting your hand out and saying, "give me," etc.) Eventually you won't need to use gestures, and soon after that you will be providing her with two-step directions. I always ask that families 'check in' on their little one's receptive language skills from time to time. You can have fun with it by playing games. (Check the activities section in this booklet for suggestions!)

# Meet Them At Their Level

In the back of this booklet is a chart of Developmental Abilities broken into two sections: Receptive Language (what your child understands from the words spoken to her) and Expressive Language (what your child is able to say or express on his own). It is important to meet your child at her level of development rather than where she "should" be in terms of her age. Examine that chart and determine where your child's skills currently fall.

If your child is two years of age but functioning at the one-year level verbally, start to think of your child's speech development as being at the one-year marker. Do not try to force him to leap from one year to two years in a single jump! We will need to take baby steps, starting where she currently is and moving every day a little closer to where she can be.

For example, if your child is stuck at the one-word sentence level but is a two or two-and-a half-year old, and you want him to start saying two-word sentences, then you will need to help him say more one-word sentences first. Modeling two or more words at a time is not going to help and will only cause frustration. Your child needs to have enough words in her vocabulary to start combining them—that can be anywhere from 25-50 words. Build the words with her first. The sentences will come later.

# It's Okay To Play Dumb

As a parent or caregiver, you are constantly being told that you know your child best, and it is true! You know the routine and how the day unfolds. You know what it means when he makes a weird sound or does a silly gesture. For the most part, you know what she wants and needs throughout the day.

So now I'm going to ask you a big favor—Pretend you *don't* know what she wants. If your child is ready to take the next step in language development, this will help her to do so.

Say your son can say one-word utterances but continues to use gestures instead of his words. In order to help him use the words he knows instead of relying on gestures, you have to play dumb. If your daughter comes into the kitchen and points to the fridge, you know she may want a snack. But play like you don't know.

You might say, "fridge." Your child keeps pointing, attempts to open the fridge. You now walk over to the fridge, hold the handle, and say, "Open?" Say it as a question, but only say the one word. Wait for your child to attempt to say the word in order to meet the request.

Attempts count! So reward any attempt he makes; it may sound like "oh" or "oh-en" or "eh eh." Those are the first steps, because any sound is better than just pointing at the fridge.

The fridge is just one example of how this can be practiced throughout the day. But be careful to not cause too much frustration. It's important to build their confidence, to reward their efforts, and to continue to provide enough support along the way. So reward frequently when attempts are made. Don't try to achieve too much at one moment, but keep encouraging your child to make it to the next level.

# The Walking-Talking Seesaw

It's also important to be aware that as your little one learns how to move and to make sounds, a "seesaw effect" may occur when he will be focused on movement only and not making sounds, or visa versa. That is, when she is very interested in crawling and maneuvering around your home, her babbling may be put on hold. Or he could be perfectly happy sitting still and babbling the day away. The seesaw can often be apparent around one year of age when he will either take those first steps or say his first words. As I always say, every child is different. Some may experience a pretty significant seesaw, and others may not experience it at all.

# Take Away Tips:

★ Think about your child in terms of her current level of functioning (where her skills fall on the developmental milestone chart).

★ Take baby steps in order to reach the next level.

★ The more baby steps you take, the easier and faster your child will learn!

★ Playing dumb is a great way to help your child take the next baby step when you feel he is ready.

# Principle #2
## Create Motivating Moments

Motivation is enormous in helping children express themselves. We need to create "motivating moments" in order to initiate your child's desire to talk. When he wants something, he will have to *do something* to get it. And that *something* is language!

Usually, food is the first thing that motivates a child. When a baby first becomes aware of feeding time and you bring a bottle or your breast into sight, she turns her head, shifts her gaze, maybe even reaches out her little arms and smiles. Your baby is essentially telling you "Yes, I want to eat." However, if your baby does not react to the bottle or breast, it's a good bet he's not hungry. Either way, you two are communicating.

Your baby is beginning to pick up the signs and signals of feeding when she hears you unsnap your bra or shake the bottle. His little brain is attuned to creating "files" in his mind that hold all of the information associated with eating. It is important for children to create these "files" so that they are able to make sense of their world. The ability to anticipate what comes next is a speech and language milestone that is critical to our wellbeing and an essential part of what makes us human.

So let's take this to the next step. Food may be the first thing that your child will label or request. Maybe your child's first and only three words are "dada," "mama," and "baba" for her bottle. That means that the bottle is a motivating item for her. Her bottle is important enough to use the word "baba" to communicate that she wants to drink milk. It's your job to determine what else motivates your child. Maybe your little one wanders over to you while you are eating. You probably end up giving him a taste of whatever you're eating once he reaches for the food. Try holding the item slightly out of reach and wait a few seconds. Does he cry? Does she continue to point or reach and say "eh eh"? If he is upset, it's probably because you have created a moment where he wants something, and he is attempting to do something to get it. Voila: you have a motivating moment.

Now, what do you do with it? If she is already quite upset, give her a small bite—it is hard to have a child do something for you once they are crying, screaming or kicking. But next time, try holding the item in front of her and saying "yum?" Say it as if you are asking a question, but only say "yum." Does he respond by smiling, reaching, or even saying, "mama" or "mm?" If he does, you need to give him that bite and jump for joy to show him you are proud.

Reward all efforts. Any verbal sound she makes to try to communicate is a step in the right direction. Your child is just learning that you want them *to say something* to *get something*. These are Baby Steps!

Motivating moments like this can be created in a variety of instances, not just with food. I like to start with treats or toys and *not* with items that are part of the daily routine, like a bottle or a safety blankie. It is easiest to start with toys or treats because they are highly motivating and not necessary to your child's daily routine. Additionally, this type of interaction with your little one works well during play activities and games.

Parents often ask me how many times a word should be modeled before they give up and give in. This is a critical question. For me, it is not about how many times you model it—it is about having your little one *do something* before getting the wanted item. That is, if you model the word five times and your child continues to just point or reach for the item and then you give up and give the item, you have just reinforced that reaching or pointing will get him what he wants. He learned that if he just keeps doing what he is doing, it works!

But you can up the ante and reward new behavior. If your child is not ready to imitate sounds or words, entice her to use a gesture before you give in. We want to make sure that we are rewarding doing something new to get something wanted. You can start teaching this new habit by having your child do something that she already knows how to do. For example, giving a high-five for a wanted toy, saying "mm" for a wanted food item, saying "mama" to have you come with him instead of just pulling you by the hand. Your little one is learning the ropes and you are helping to praise her efforts. Continue these moments throughout your day as it feels natural, comfortable, and most importantly, not intrusive.

# The Clear Bag Technique...
# Make 'Em Work For It

While clear plastic bags are an incredible invention for food preservation, they are also tops when it comes to creating motivating moments. Let's give it a try.

This technique is an example of the broader concept of "gentle withholding." That is, you are holding onto an item or holding off on performing an action until your child *does something* in order to receive it. Wherever I am working, my toys are in clear bags or containers. I have individual clear plastic bags full of each one of my activities: one bag full of Thomas and friends and tracks. One full of dolls. One bag of pretend food. The bags are all closed. The idea is for the child to be able to see what's inside (and hopefully be motivated by the item). He should not be able to open the bag on his own. I may pull one of my containers out and show the child, "Oh look, Thomas and his friends! They came to play!" The child may reach for the bag or may even try to grab the items. Depending on her level, I will redirect that behavior. I will have her gently point to the bag and use one word ("Thomas") to request it. As the child's skills develop, we'll work on using two words for the request ("want Thomas"), and so on. I like to start one baby step above the child's current level. If your child is not ready to take that baby step, then jump back down to what you know he can do.

Keep in mind, it's very important NOT to reward bad behavior. We do not want to give in to whining, yelling, hitting, grabbing, or any other non-preferred action. When you give your child what she wants following her bad behavior, you reward and reinforce the very behavior you do not want.

If you give your child a wanted item after he screamed for it, then next time he wants something, he's likely to scream to get it. The best way to get around this is to step back. Have her do something—anything—that is preferred before giving the wanted item. For example, you can walk away and say, "Let me know when you are ready." Or you can say, "Show me a calm body and you can have X." You can also have her perform an action that she can consistently do before giving X. ("Give me a high-five for X.")

Once the child does something to get the bag, he will likely be unable to open it, which is where more work comes into play. He may become frustrated and throw the bag, hit the bag, or give it back to you. This is where you model what you want the magic words to be. "Want open?" "Open please." "Open." "Help." "Need help." "Want help." "Help me." I switch it up based on what I need to work on with that particular child on that particular day. However, as mentioned before, take baby steps. Start with gestures (pointing to the bag). Move to one-word sentences ("open"). And so on.

The clear bag technique raises the question of how the child's environment may be affecting her communication. Are most things in your home easily accessible? Can she reach most preferred foods, toys, and activities on her own? I ask this question to all of my parents because oftentimes your child does not necessarily have to interact with you in order to maneuver throughout her day. He may be able to easily retrieve anything without the need for help. I have experienced two-year olds who have intricate systems that involve multiple furniture pieces and some big climbs in order to gain access to food and drink in the kitchen and/or activities in their room. This is a clear sign that it's *easier* for your child to build, climb, and take physical risks rather than to walk over to you and use a gesture, a one-word request, or a two-word request. I think most of us would agree that it is preferable to help children work for it by using their words instead of engaging in tricky maneuvers that may result in a fall.

You are in charge of how to help your child rely on language in order to maneuver through the environment and retrieve wanted items. For example, you might want to put a few preferred objects in clear containers. Maybe you move preferable food and drink to higher shelves or out of sight. We don't want to frustrate your child too much, so don't change an environment in which your child is able to touch, grab and take everything to making sure absolutely *nothing* is accessible. Remember, baby steps! Start small.

Once you make a few changes, it's important to follow up. You have changed the game and your child needs to be informed of the new rules. Do you want him to point to the wanted item in order for you to retrieve it? Then you have to model this behavior a few times, be patient, show him how to point by gently using your hand to guide him, and then give in immediately after he demonstrates the behavior. (Giving in means giving the wanted item. Make sure you are willing to give him the wanted item before you show him what to do in order to retrieve it.) Remember to meet your child at her level. If she has no words, practice gestures such as pointing. If she is at the one-word level, practice a variety of one-word sentences. And keep going.

***Side Note:** When demonstrating pointing, continue to label the item that is being requested using one word to describe that item. That way, your child is hearing the appropriate label for the item with each demonstration and is more likely to use that word in order to request when he is ready!*

# Take Away Tips:

★ Your child needs to learn that she needs to *do something* in order to *get something*. That *something* is communication—pointing, gesturing, babbling, attempting to say a word, or saying a three-word phrase, depending on the child's developmental level.

★ The more motivated your child is by a task or wanted item, the more likely he is to use language.

★ You can help by using gentle withholding (clear bags, higher shelves, not giving in to a request.)

★ Start with toys or treats, not items that are a part of the daily routine.

★ Reinforce and reward new behaviors, gestures, and language so that your little one learns that she has to do something to get something.

# Principle #3
## Consistency, Consistency, Consistency

As with the majority of aspects in your child's life, <u>consistency is crucial for learning</u>. The more consistent you are in the expectations set up for your child, the more easily and readily she will be able to figure out the rules and play along. I cannot tell you the exact times when you should be practicing the tips that I have mentioned above because I do not know your routine. However, if you remain as consistent as possible in your choices, then it will be an easy transition for you and your child.

That is, if you are going to practice the concept of "open" when your child needs help opening something, then do so every single time. Unless there are tears or strong emotion—you will not be able to create a motivating moment during those times. You can use "open" with your clear bags of toys, the fridge, food, and any door. The more consistent you are with your expectations, the more consistent your child will be with using his language.

Children are context learners, meaning they initially learn a new skill within the bubble of a specific scenario. For example, saying "cheese" when she is sitting in her high chair during lunchtime with you, her caregiver modeling the word and showing her a preferred piece of orange cheese, may be a familiar context. However, if she goes in another room to play and a sibling says "cheese" while playing in the pretend kitchen, she may not understand that the yellow, hard, plastic object her sibling shows her is also "cheese" and should be labeled as such. Maintaining consistent language in the various routine contexts throughout your day will give your child the support he needs during a time in his life when he is absorbing so much.

While we're on the topic of consistency, let's talk about behavior. Toddlers can be tricky and we need to be prepared for selective listening and the words "mine" and "no." I often see a good deal of frustration from children who are unable to clearly communicate their wants and needs. Most of our tiny friends want to feel independent and in control—and there is a pretty easy fix for that: Consistently provide choices!

When given a choice, your child feels in control, yet you are providing the specific options that you feel good about. Most importantly, when you provide choices, your child is less likely to say, "no." Instead of saying, "Take your shoes off" or "Are you ready to take off your shoes?" you can change it up: "You can take off your shoes by yourself or I can help you—you pick!" Instead of asking, "Do you want to eat breakfast?" you can say, "You can have eggs or a waffle for breakfast." Or: "It's time for breakfast, your choices are on the table - you pick!" This method helps your little one feel in control and less frustrated. The more consistent you are about providing choices, the faster they will become a part of your daily routine.

# Be A Broken Record

The title of this section—"be a broken record"—is my own form of self-mockery. I am chalk full of Molly-isms that I repeat on a daily basis. Repetition is an important part of the learning process for all children (and adults). When learning a new thing, it is important to provide numerous chances for that "aha!" moment to occur. This section also touches on what we went over earlier in the Motivating Moments sections; anticipation of what will happen next is an essential milestone.

Here are some of my favorite sayings to show how simple, repetitive language is the easiest way to teach hard concepts. Communication is a key part of being human. Think about it: for most grown-ups, the biggest source of relationship frustration comes from communication, whether it's with a colleague, a spouse, a boss, or a friend. Teaching your child how essential it is to listen and to be a kind and appropriate communicator is an enormous feat! We are doing ourselves a favor by breaking communication down into a simplistic, easy-to-teach, easy-to-follow, and easy-to-repeat practice.

**Listening Ears:** I teach listening ears early (this can start around 12-18 months of age). Your child is born into a world where he is essentially being told things all day long. Some things he loves listening to and other things—like "no, it's not time for that," "maybe another day," "don't touch that," or "give it to me" —he isn't too fond of. However, it is important to teach your child that she has two ears that are in charge of listening. It should always start off as a fun game.

Here is how it looks: you give a direction, tell your child no, for example, and he doesn't respond. You say, "Hmm your listening ears must not be turned on! Let me check them." You go over and pretend to push a very important, some may even say magical, button behind each of his ears. "Ah, now your listening ears are on! Let's try again." Then you proceed to help him out with whatever he was supposed to do in the first place before his ears were 'turned on.' As your child grows, you will simply say, "listening ears" each time you need him to complete a task or follow your direction.

The reason that I like the game is that it provides your child with a chance to have a do-over. Say she isn't picking up the toy that was thrown across the floor. Instead of immediately getting in trouble for not listening, she gets a second chance. You as mom, dad, or caregiver say, "Oh your listening ears must not be turned on" and then you go through the routine to allow her a second chance to comply. Eventually, you will just say, "listening ears" with that all-too-familiar facial expression to match. When your little one gets it, you can reward listening ears with stickers, treats, a fun game, a big hug, a high-five, or a compliment.

**Asking Words:** These are the words we use instead of snatching something from someone's hand, using demanding, give-me language, whining for an item, or any other behavior your child may be using instead of requesting items with her words. We also learn early that "we do not use grabbing hands," but need to use "asking words" instead. Asking words can be as simple as saying the label of the item ("ball"), using a two-word sentence ("ball please" or "want ball"), or as advanced and preferred as "Can I have ball, please?" a phrase I work on with my three-to-five year olds. But remember, please, baby steps are the biggest steps!

**"Please" is Not the Magic Word:** The word "please" is *not* the awesome one-word sentence that it is believed to be. If you are constantly modeling "please" while holding a variety of different objects, then you are teaching your child to say "please" and only "please" in order to receive anything. You may create the most well-mannered kid on the block, but his vocabulary will be lacking! Your child may start to say please to request any and all things, when it is more valuable for her to learn a variety of labels for things in her environment. Save working on "please" until you are at the two-word sentence level or above, and when your child has developed a robust vocabulary.

**Telling Words:** These are the words that children use that sound too demanding (e.g. "give me that"). The reality is, adults are much more likely to give in to requests when children use kind asking words instead of demanding telling words. When I hear, "Give me that" I model, "Can I have?" and have the child imitate the preferred phrase before I hand the item over. *It is important to note that I switched an unfriendly 3-word phrase for a kind 3-word phrase—staying on the child's level!*

**Looking Eyes:** It's important for your child to be making eye contact with you when you're having a conversation. It's also important to ensure he maintains appropriate attention to the task at hand. Eye contact is the best way to ensure you have an engaged little one.

**Have-To's:** As much as we want our children to feel that they have choices throughout their day, there are certain things that are Have-To's. Each parent will need to decide what the

Have-To's are in the household. They might be washing hands, brushing teeth, or sitting down for meals. You will be giving your child a serious leg up if you teach these skills and concepts early, as the school environment (even preschool) will come with many Have-To's. The more you are able to provide choices throughout the day, the easier it will be for your child to comply with the Have-To's.

**Calm Body:** This is a tough one! The sensory system for a child under five is still growing and evolving. This makes it hard for a child to sit still, speak at an appropriate volume, focus on one task at a time, and so on. I say, "calm body" when I think a child needs to reset and relax in order to bring himself to a centered and balanced state in which learning can occur. Yes, high expectations! Many kids may need assistance in order to maintain a calm body. Perhaps doing some jumping jacks first will help. Maybe they need a huge, deep, bear hug. Some may need to sit on your lap, or to take a deep breath. You know your child best, so start with good, old-fashioned trial and error. Look out for moments when she seems most calm. What did she do right before? What does the environment feel like? You can always jot down some behaviors for a few days and see what you find.

**I'm Here When You're Ready:** This phrase has layers! First off, I want every child that I work with to truly feel that I am *here*. By that I mean: I am present, on his team, available, accepting, and supportive. Secondly, I need him to be ready for me. Ready means calm and engaged. If a child is tantruming, then she is not ready and will not be able to see or hear me. This phrase is powerful because I am demonstrating that I am a constant that will remain here, and when she returns to a calm state, she will be able to see and hear me again!

# Take Away Tips:

★ It is important to be consistent in your behavior in order to help your child learn!

★ Children learn within contexts, so if you are consistent across a variety of contexts then more learning will occur.

★ Providing your child with clear and consistent choices throughout the day will decrease frustration and improve behavior.

★ Simple and repetitive phrases are extremely helpful, especially when teaching BIG concepts.

# Activities

Now let us put all of this wonderful information to good use! This section includes simple things that you can do with your child during your normal daily routine. You are busy, and I know it! The purpose is for these activities to feel natural, fun, and easy for you and your child. These interchangeable ideas are just a starting point to get the ball rolling for you and your child.

## Getting-Dressed Activities

The good news about getting dressed, is that you do it at least two times per day. Even changing a diaper and potty training are considered getting-dressed activities.

★ **Let's Label!** Label only the items that you are using as you get dressed. For example, only say, "diaper," "t-shirt," "pants," "socks," "brush," "bow," or "hat." It is important for your child to have a multisensory learning experience for labels. That is, she sees the clothing item, touches the item, smells the item, and hears the item's label. All of this happens in the split second when you grab a diaper, show it to your child, and say the word "diaper." When multiple senses are involved, the learning experience is strengthened.

★ **Use Simple Language** such as, "put on" and "take off" during dressing time. These two phrases expose your child to two-word phrases combining action words (put and take) with prepositions or spatial words (on and off). Again, your child is experiencing these words within the context of actually getting dressed, which enhances her ability to learn.

★ **Don't Forget About Descriptors!** Take advantage of the wide array of adjectives to build your child's vocabulary. Clothing items come in a variety of colors, textures, sizes, lengths, and shapes. Depending on your child's level, you may be labeling and teaching a descriptor word ("blue"), or perhaps increasing your child's phrase length (he says "blue" and you say "blue shirt"). Maybe you ask a who/what/where question ("what color is your shirt?"), or you have him follow a direction ("give me blue shirt"). All of it adds up to a bigger vocabulary and better communication.

# "Tubby Time" Activities

★ **Body Parts!** All body parts are exposed during the bath-time routine. As you wash your child's body parts, label them as you go. Focus on two to four parts at each bath and don't add new body parts until your child is able to identify and label the parts on her own. Start with body parts that are easy: head, eyes, nose, mouth, ears, tummy, hands, toes, and knees. End the bath with a "slow review." That is, go back and touch the two to four parts you focused on slowly and simply. (Touch and label, then pause. Touch and label, then pause. Repeat).

★ **Feel It All!** The bath is a sensory experience and a great time to focus on sensory words. Practice "wet" vs. "dry" as you go in and out of the bath; or "fast" vs. "slow" as you splash the water; or "big" vs. "small" as you compare your body to theirs ("big hand" vs. "small hand"). But remember, only practice big vs. small body parts with body parts that your little one has already mastered!

★ **Play Time!** The bath can be a time of great imagination and play—whether you have a million bath toys or none, you can get creative, like popping soap bubbles. Bubbles are amazing because the words "bubble" and "pop" are relatively easy first words for your child to say. Bubbles also go "up" and "down," which are concepts that are easy for your child to see, experience, and learn in the bath. You can also practice "more," which is an awesome first word that can be used in a variety of contexts.

# Meal Time Activities

★ **Eat and Repeat!** We tend to use the same vocabulary words over and over during meals. We have the classics: "eat," "all done," and "more." Then we have more mature words: "pour," "mix," "shake," "spoon," "fork," and "knife." Lastly, we have advanced words: "thank you" and "please." The classics are a good starting point. The mature words should begin when your child has a more diverse vocabulary of around 50 words, and the advanced come into play when your child reaches the two-word sentence level.

★ **Folks, We Have a Motivator!** Food is motivating for the majority of kids, so you can really build vocabulary here. Label all food items as you prepare a meal if your child is watching, and then throughout the meal as you eat. You can even use some gentle withholding—that is, your child points to a cookie, you hold the cookie and label it simply, "cookie." Now you wait for your child to attempt to label it herself, but be sure to give the cookies once any attempt has been made!

★ **Let 'Em Choose!** Meals are a good time to present choices. You can pick two or three items that are appropriate for the meal and have your child pick the one he wants to eat. If your child is not yet verbal, simply have her point to the wanted item when you present the choices. Just remember to also provide a simple label for the item that you will work towards producing once your child is ready. For example, your child may not yet be able to say "spaghetti," but you could work for "noodle" or "pasta."

# Playtime Activities

★ **Picture Books:** Start with simple books with a single picture per page. Point with your finger to the picture and say a one-word label ("train"). To test your child's comprehension, say, "show me train" and have him point to the picture. Practice labeling items in the book by pointing to the item, saying the label and then pausing to look at your child to see if she is ready to attempt the imitation. I love starting with books that incorporate touch and feel or have other sensory components that encourage interaction, such as Velcro books, felt books, books with moving pieces, pop-up or peek-a-boo books. Motivation is important because it promotes joint attention—that is, when your child is focused on both a task (the book) and you. Joint attention is necessary for learning. This is as simple as your baby looking at the book, then looking at you, and then back at the book. Interactive books do a lot of the work of keeping your child engaged. They are usually full of directions for our tiny friends to follow, such as "find the cow," or "look under the table." They promote expressive language as well. Since your child will be engaged and demonstrating joint attention, you are likely to hear new sounds and words when you read together! Lastly, books are a great way to teach turn taking, which is an important skill needed for both play and language/conversation. Musical books or those with singsong verses also provide wonderful opportunities for our little ones to fill in the blank and finish a sentence for you. When you add a melodic intonation to a phrase, your child is more likely to imitate you. This is because you are inviting the right brain to help with a left-brain task, which is best explained as using two hands instead of one to carry a heavy box.

★ **Animals:** Animal sounds come first, so you can provide your child with both the label and sound (for example: "cow" and "moo"). It is perfectly normal for your child to pick up a cow and say, "moo" before she labels "cow." You can also practice your who/what/where questions by asking, "What does the cow say?" and having your child make the sound. Once she has both the label and the sound, ask, "Who says moo?" A more advanced step for three-to-five year olds would be categorizing animals based on where they live—farm animals, zoo animals, ocean animals, etc. You can ask "Where?" questions once you have taught the concept.

★ **The Imitation Game:** When starting the imitation game, start with actions. It is usually easier for children to imitate actions or gestures rather than sounds or words. Sit across from your child and start with some good old-fashioned trial and error! Put your arms up, stick your tongue out, clap your hands, touch your nose, etc. If your little one imitates some actions and not others, keep going with those that are successful and make a little game out of it. It's important to get excited to show your child that you want him to copy you. We want to reinforce this wonderful new behavior. Once your child imitates actions and gestures, move on to sounds. Often kids prefer to imitate silly, nonsensical sounds at first (a raspberry sound, gibberish sounds.) These sounds are more likely to be imitated if you add changing intonations and a funny face to match.

Additionally, know that vowel sounds come before consonants because they are easier to produce. Vowels simply require opening and closing your mouth different degrees and rounding your lips--or not. (Try it: say "ah," "oooh," "oh," "ee," "eh," and feel your mouth and lips change.)

However, consonants require contact between two parts of your mouth such as your lips, teeth, tongue, and/or the roof of your mouth (Try it: You will need both of your lips to produce b, p, or m. You will need your teeth and your bottom lip to produce f or v. The tongue and roof of your mouth are necessary to produce k or g sounds.) I hope you just had a nice little mouth workout!

So we start with imitating vowels because they are easier. Moreover, vowels that are easy for your little one to see are the easiest (e.g. an exaggerated "oooh" sound with rounded lips; a big open mouth for "ah," etc.)

When your child is successful imitating vowel sounds, you can start adding consonants. Start with those that you have heard your little one use before. Typical beginning consonants include but are not limited to: m, n, p, b, and d. I find it's easiest to start with simple consonant-vowel combinations such as, "mama" "dah" "boo," etc. Once you are ready to take a baby step forward, try simple one-syllable words, then two-syllable words, and so on.

# Outside Activities

★ **Outside Labels:** Whether you are walking to the bus, driving in a car, or playing in the yard there are some basic "outside labels" that you should be able to see, touch, hear, and show your child. "Car," "bus," "tree," "grass," "sky," "plane," "dog," "bird," and so on. These are pretty typical first words for a lot of children because they tend to see them over and over. The more exposure you give, the more readily your child will start to label on her own. Once he has the labels down, you can expand the concept. For example, when I talk about planes I sing a little song that goes: "flying, flying in the sky." I am expanding on where planes go and how they move, which are things we talk about whenever we see a plane.

★ **'I SPY'** is a classic game because it's fun, and more importantly, it works! The game can begin with you naming something that you spy, "I spy a truck," and have your child identify the item by pointing to it or reaching toward it. (* Be sure your child is able to identify the item before asking him to find it! *) You can make the game more complex by giving hints: "I spy something yellow" or "I spy something big." This introduces descriptive concepts like color and size. Your child will ready to be the spy when she is at the one-word level. You will start by saying the carrier phrase, "I spy..." and let her fill in what she spies using her own one-word label (e.g. "baby," "cheese," "cat," etc.)

★ **Following the Leader:** It is important to practice following directions within the context of play. Some of my favorite activities include but are not limited to: Simon Says, scavenger hunts, obstacle courses, movement songs with directions (i.e. Going on a Bear Hunt, Sesame Street Usher's ABC's, We are the Dinosaurs, If You're Happy and You Know It, etc.) and games like, The Cat in The Hat, I Can Do That. Remember to start with simple one-step directions and provide your little one with the support necessary to be successful. For example, he may need some physical help completing the direction at first (i.e. you taking his hand to help him perform a task.) Visuals may be helpful, or even verbal hints. Baby steps are always key!

# Cocktail Party Advice

When I tell people that I am a speech language pathologist, it is often an open invitation for a question and answer panel, which I absolutely love! I always preface these conversations with the same disclaimer: * If you are truly concerned about your child's speech or language skills, then you should have him or her assessed by a licensed speech language pathologist and go from there.*

But that is no fun at a cocktail party...so here is my go-to advice for specific issues:

## Stuttering:

★ Do not interrupt your child.

★ After your child finishes telling you something that involved stuttering, say, "That was a little bumpy. Let's try saying it together."

★ Say the phrase in a singsong fashion. (Singing something instead of saying it brings the right brain in on a left-brain task.)

★ It will also be fun for your child to sing it, as it's a new task and kids love songs!

★ My best piece of advice is to not bring too much attention to the fact that your child may be stuttering.

★ Stuttering can be typical for kids between three and five years of age—their motor movements are not fully coordinated so it is an appropriate phase that some children go through.

# ARTICULATION:

★ Saying the /f/ sound can be challenging for many children. I call this the "bunny sound" because you need to put your front teeth on your bottom lip and then blow air out in order to make the sound. First practice saying the /f/ sound by yourself before you start to work with your child so you know how it feels and what it looks like. Next, grab your child and get in front of a mirror and practice being bunnies! All you need to do is get the front teeth onto the bottom lip and blow out air. You need to make sure your child can see you doing the sound the whole time—and really over exaggerate! I always have a picture of a cartoon bunny with his teeth on his bottom lip to reinforce the point and the fun.

★ Saying the /th/ sound: This is the "tongue sandwich sound" because you need to make sure your tongue is sandwiched in between your top and bottom teeth. After you have the correct placement, you want to follow the same directions as above with the /f/ sound and blow your air out gently.

★ Saying the /s/ sound: This is the "snake sound" because you are hissing like a snake. I am assuming that your child is lisping and placing his tongue between the top and bottom teeth and then blowing air out. In order to correct that lisping sound, you need to help your child bring her tongue back so that it is behind the front teeth and then blow air out. Snake pictures DO NOT help here since they usually have a tongue OUT of the mouth when we want the tongue BEHIND the teeth. Again it is important for you to practice first and use a mirror!

★ Saying the /r/ sound: I call this the "growl sound." But all I will say on the /r/ is to practice growling with your child (i.e. the grrrrr kind!) because you truly need to be a trained speech language pathologist in order to properly teach the /r/ sound. Growls do help though!

★ Articulation, for the most part, should not be "worked on" with children under the age of three. Give your child enough time to develop strong language skills before thinking about how clear their speech is. Additionally, always practice the sound in isolation first. That is, you are saying the sound by itself and not in a word (e.g. just practice "sss" not "sock" etc.)

# DROOLING:

★ Hum! Humming promotes a closed mouth and if your mouth is closed, you won't be drooling.

★ Wipe your child's mouth starting beneath the bottom lip up toward the top lip in order to promote a nice, closed-mouth posture.

★ A closed-mouth posture is important because it means that your child is appropriately breathing from the nose and it will decrease the chance of drool escaping.

★ Have your little one wear a sweatband on her wrist and remind her to wipe her own mouth throughout the day. If we allow him to have a wet mouth all day, he won't be able to feel the difference between wet and dry anymore. The goal is to help her feel when her chin starts to become wet on her own.

★ Give your child simple reminders throughout the day to either "take a big swallow" or "close lips." I use different phrases with different children depending on what feels most natural. Some little ones respond best when I tell them to "catch it." This means that saliva has built up onto their bottom lip, but there is still time to catch it and swallow before it drips down to the chin.

★ It is important to check in with the ENT if you believe your child is excessively drooling and/or mouth breathing.

# How To Reach Out For Help

If you believe that your child needs speech language therapy, you should start by discussing your concerns with your child's pediatrician. If you child is in school, you can also consult with the teacher. You will be able to receive a FREE evaluation from your county by contacting the appropriate representative. Your pediatrician and/or child's school will be able to point you in the right direction. <u>Please remember that the earlier you reach out, the better!</u> It is better to be informed than wondering whether or not there is an issue at hand.

# APPENDIX:

## DEVELOPMENTAL ABILITIES

## Understanding Speech & Language Milestones

Speech language pathologists will often talk about milestones, those markers on a developmental journey of where a child is and what is appropriate at what age. While the below list of milestones is not comprehensive, I simply want you to gain a basic idea of the skills that your child may start to demonstrate at different ages.

It is critical to remember that each child is unique and will grow at his own pace. It is even more critical to know that with the right help early on, every child can reach her maximum potential. I list these milestones not to point out where and how your child may be behind the curve, but to give us a road map of what activities are developmentally appropriate and to give us an idea of where extra work might be needed.

# FIRST WE WILL LOOK AT MILESTONES FOR RECEPTIVE LANGUAGE. THIS IS YOUR CHILD'S UNDERSTANDING OF LANGUAGE.

**These are the Receptive Language Milestones we look for in a child from birth to six months of age. Your child:**

- ★ Looks back at you when you look at her

- ★ Looks at the person who is talking

- ★ Turns his head to different sounds (environmental sounds and voices)

- ★ Responds to her name being called

- ★ Relaxes and smiles in response to familiar and soothing voices

- ★ Notices music and toys that make sounds

- ★ Displays excitement (i.e. kicking, smiling, etc.) with favorite toys

- ★ Understands differences in your tone—when you're angry, happy, sad—and demonstrates this understanding by changing her facial expressions and/or his body movements

**From six months to one year, your child:**

- ★ Understands games such as peek-a-boo

- ★ Stops an activity when his name is called

- ★ Responds to 'bye bye' or 'hi' with a gesture, like waving

★ Starts to follow simple directions with gestures. For example, if you say, "Give me" and hold your hand out, the child will give you the item. If you say, "Come here" with a waving gesture, the child comes over.

★ Looks at familiar objects in a room—like a cup, ball, shoe—when you name them

★ Understands when told "no"

★ Responds to music with facial expressions and movements

## From one to two years, the child:

★ Responds to simple, routine directions without gestures, such as "Grab blankie," "Find your cup," "Give me kisses."

★ Starts to point to basic body parts when prompted. "Where's your nose?" "Where are your eyes?" "Show me your tummy."

★ Starts to point to familiar pictures in books (dog, ball)

★ Finds familiar objects in the room that are named

★ Starts to understand simple who/what/where questions. Such as "Where are your shoes?" "What does a dog say?"

★ Understands around 50 words

## From two to three years, a child:

★ Points to pictures in books more consistently

★ Responds to more WH questions that are within context ("Where is your teddy bear?" "Who is in the car?" "What are you eating?")

★ Points to more body parts (e.g. mouth, head, hands, feet)

★ Understands "in" "on" "out" "off" in simple directions, "put in the trash," "turn light on.")

★ Understands simple concepts such as, "big" "small" "up" "down," etc.

★ Follows two-step related directions ("Go find your socks and bring them to mommy.")

★ Understands pronouns "me" "you" "my" "your" ("Touch MY nose" vs. "Touch YOUR nose.")

## From three to four years, a child:

★ Follows two-step unrelated directions. For example: "Put your apple in the garbage and then go get your pajamas."

★ Understands simple WH questions that are abstract or out of context ("Where do pigs live?" "Who drives the bus?")

★ Understands object function ("What do we wear on our feet?" etc.)

★ Understands pronouns "he," "she," "they," etc.

★ Understands simple prepositions (under, on top, etc.)

## From four to five years, a child:

★ Answers questions about daily activities (e.g. "What did you do at school today?" etc.)

★ Understands rhymes & sing-song phrases

★ Understands most WH questions (who, what, where, when, why, how)

★ Understands more prepositions (e.g. in front, behind, next to, etc.)

★ From five to six years, a child:

★ Understands time words such as, "now," "before," "after," "today," "tomorrow," "yesterday"

★ Follows three-step directions ("First take your shoes off, then put your clothes in the hamper, and last wash your hands.")

★ Understands short paragraphs

★ Understands "if," "because," and "when"

★ Understands more complex sentences (e.g. passive phrases: "the monkey was fed a banana" etc.)

# Now let's consider Expressive Language. This is what your child says. Here are the relevant milestones.

**From birth to six months, your child:**

★ Makes "happy" sounds (gurgles, coos) and "not-so-happy" sounds (crying, fussing)

★ Smiles

★ Giggles and laughs

★ Makes sounds in response to being talked to

★ Babbles sounds: p, b, d, h, w, m (usually)

★ Squeals, growls, and makes raspberries

## From six months to one year, your child:

★ Babbles even more sounds: p, b, t, d, h, w, n, m (usually)

★ Takes turns making sounds and mimicking a conversation

★ Starts to shake his head to indicate "no"

★ Says "uh oh" (or a different version) to indicate something did not go the way it was expected to

★ Tries to imitate your sounds and mouth movements

★ Uses gestures to communicate, like clapping, waving, or lifting arms to be picked up.

## From one to two years, your child:

★ Makes animal sounds— "moo," for a cow, "baah," for a sheep

★ Uses jargon: the production of syllable strings with appropriate, adult-like inflection. This is the child's own little language.

★ Makes sounds while gesturing to request items, like pointing and saying "eh eh"

★ Imitates simple words ("ball," "bubble," etc.)

★ Names familiar objects around her

★ Greets when asked (e.g. "Say hi.")

★ Labels a few pictures in a book

★ Starts to name body parts ("eye," "nose," "tummy")

★ Starts to hum and sing

★ Says "no" (and never, ever stops)

★ Says up to 10 words (around 12-18 months)

★ Says up to 20 words (around 18-24 months)

★ Says between 50-100 words (around 24 months)

★ Imitates and uses two-word combinations ("hi mama")

## From two to three years:

★ Starts to use word combinations more readily ("more juice," "mama up," "bye dada," "that my ball")

★ Names more body parts

★ Names objects in environment and pictures in books

★ Says around 200 words

★ Starts saying pronouns (but probably not accurately). These include: "me," "my," and "you"

★ Starts to use prepositions "on," "in," "under"

★ Starts to narrate play with toys

## From three to four years:

★ Produces simple sentences ("I eat banana." "Daddy at work.")

★ Asks What, Where, and Who questions

★ Talks about what happened during the day

★ Starts to use plurals ("babies," "cats")

★ Starts to use 'ing' words ("running," "eating")

★ Says up to 1,000 words!

★ Uses sentences of four or more words

★ Uses "I," "you," "me" correctly

★ Uses more verbs

## Four to five years:

- ★ Starts to use more pronouns correctly ("he," "she," "they," "her," "his," etc.)

- ★ Starts to use more prepositions correctly ("next to," "behind," etc.)

- ★ Speaks like a tiny adult with minor grammatical errors

- ★ Says most consonants (but may have difficulty with: l, s, z, r, f, v, ch, sh, th, j)

- ★ Holds simple conversations

- ★ Tells short stories

- ★ Changes voice depending on the situation (i.e. talking louder outside than inside, speaking differently to a baby or a pet)

## Five to six years:

- ★ Talks like a tiny grown up

- ★ Converses easily with adults and other children

- ★ Starts to use past and future verb tenses

- ★ Uses adjectives and adverbs

# Sample Charts For Tracking

## Simple Word Count

| Date: | Word: |
|---|---|
| 6/28 | "meh" for milk |
| 6/28 | "mama" |
| 6/29 | "bye bye" |

## How Words Are Said

| Imitated Words: | Spontaneous Words: |
|---|---|
| "More" | "No" |

## Word Types

| Nouns | Verbs | Pronouns | Adjectives | Prepositions |
|---|---|---|---|---|
| "ball" | "go" | "me" | "big" | "on" |
| "cup" | "want" | "mine" | | "off" |
| "baby" | | | | |

## Following Directions

| Type: | 1-Step | 2-Step | 3-Step |
|---|---|---|---|
| | "Give me" | "Go get your shoes and bring them to me" | "First take off your coat, then hang up your backpack, and last put your shoes in the bucket" |
| | "Find your cup" | "Bring your plate to the sink and rinse it off" | |

# Stay In Touch

**Learn more at** www.thespeechteacher123.com

**Follow Molly Dresner on:**

- ★ **Instagram:** @thespeechteacher
- ★ **Facebook:** facebook.com/thespeechteacher123
- ★ **Pinterest:** pinterest.com/thespeechteacher
- ★ Reach out by emailing her at thespeechteacher123@gmail.com

Made in the USA
Columbia, SC
04 June 2019